A REINHOLD CRAFT PAPERBACK

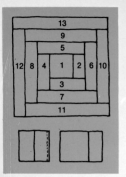
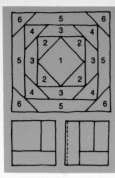

ELSIE SVENNAS

- Designs
- Material
- Technique

Patchcraft

Patchcraft

Patchcraft

designs
material
technique

Elsie Svennas

VAN NOSTRAND REINHOLD COMPANY
New York   Cincinnati   Toronto   London   Melbourne

This book was originally
published in Swedish under the
title *Lek Med Lappar* by
I. C. A. Förlaget, Västeràs, Sweden

Copyright © Elsie Svennås and
I. C. A. Förlaget, Västeràs, 1971
English translation © Van
Nostrand Reinhold Company Ltd. 1972

Photography — Georg Sessle
Sven-Eric Sjöström, Ro
Alkhagen, Folke Johansso
Herbert Andersso

This book is set in Univers and
printed in Great Britain b
Jolly & Barber Limited, Rugt
and bound by Richard Clay (Tl
Chaucer Press) Ltd, Bunga
Suffo

Published by Van Nostra
Reinhold Company, Ir
450 West 33rd St., New Yo
N.Y. 10001 and Van Nostra
Reinhold Company Lt
Windsor House, 46 Victo
Street, London S.W

Published simultaneously
Canada by Van Nostra
Reinhold Company L

16   15   14   13   12   11   10   9   8   7   6   5   4   3   2

Contents

Introduction

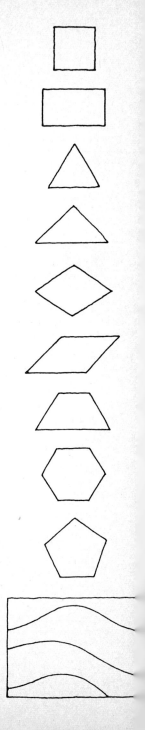

In museums there are many examples of beautiful quilts and draperies consisting entirely of patches sewn together. Nowadays we have no need to save scraps to keep ourselves warm or decorate the house: modern affluence and mass production have seen to that. Our interest in patchwork lies mainly in its intriguing visual effects and in the satisfaction that comes from making something beautiful, individual and useful — not to mention economical.

Most of us probably already have a 'bit' box of pieces of material left over from discarded or worn-out clothes, kitchen cloths and bed linen (if you haven't such 'bits' they can usually be supplied by a friend or the remnant counter or even bought by the pound from clothing factories) and this haphazard collection can be put to work in patches to create something unusual and worthwhile — perhaps even to give expression to artistic talent.

In the same way as an artist works with colours so you too can start to work with patches. Sometimes, just rummaging among the pieces of material is enough to discover that certain patterns and colours go well together and others don't. Many of the models shown in this book would not have turned out so well if their creator had decided to go out and buy each piece of material separately. But do not delay the completion of your project for want of a few patches: then is the time to go out and buy remnants of material or dye light-coloured pieces you already have. Bits of ribbon and lace will also come in useful.

This book gives suggestions on how you can 'play' with your patches; how you can design patterns, both representative and abstract. It describes not only how to 'paint' with patches but also the more traditional patchwork techniques: the latter may be regarded as 'rules of the game' — and indeed, for many people such rules are a great help. You may decide, for instance, to stitch patches together in a certain regular form or to sew an appliqué with patches in a certain way or with a certain seam. These traditional methods of work and techniques will be most helpful to the beginner, though the expert, familiar both with the material and techniques may sometimes prefer to try out new combinations and to discover different ways of constructing his or her project. Just as new materials are continually being created and our demands change, so the possibilities of patchwork are inexhaustible and each one of us, whether beginner or expert, can readily produce an individual result.

Obviously, some projects take longer than others, depending on the size of the project, the size and shape of the patches, and whether the patches are stitched by hand or machine. If you are a beginner, start on a small project using the simplest technique, that is, stitching patches together in a simple, regular shape or into a 'mosaic' pattern, using the same shape and size for all the patches. As you progress, more complicated projects can be tackled involving, perhaps, an irregular shaped patch or a difficult material to work with. It is rather like making jigsaw puzzles — only for patchwork the larger the pieces the more difficult the adjustment of colour and design.

The most traditional patchwork is based on the hexagonal shape, and it is with this we start, describing the basic technique of the craft and showing how various effects can be obtained. But first, a word about materials and equipment.

tractive wall decoration
th centre of hexagons
wn together in a mosaic
ttern. Note the pleasing
ernation between dark,
ht and lined flowers.
e pattern is appliquéd on
etched fabric.

Materials and Equipment

Materials

As suggested in the introduction, anything goes and any bits of leftover material may be used — providing, of course, they are large enough for the individual patches you have in mind. Cottons, linens, hessian, man-made fibres such as nylon and terylene, silks, even velvets and satins may be used. Obviously some materials are more difficult to work with than others and are best hoarded until you have gained a little experience, but in general, any material you can think of will find a niche for itself in patchwork. The one type of material best avoided is the one which *frays* badly, as fraying makes it difficult, if not impossible, to join the patches together satisfactorily. Another word of warning: while you can use just about any material, you cannot use many different materials together in the same project. If you are planning to mix your materials take great care to choose only those of the same texture and strength; never, for example, use cotton and silk together or the result will be a disaster.

Always pre-shrink *all* materials before use (remember, even ribbons and edging can shrink) — do not wait until your project is finished and thrown into the wash-tub or the result will be a hotch-potch of different size patches and all your careful work will be ruined. As a rule, it is best to dry-clean patchwork articles to avoid any possible deterioration of your precious handiwork, but if you intend to wash it (for example, if you are making a child's garment which will need constant cleaning), be sure also to test each different piece of material for colour fastness before use. The question of colour itself will be dealt with under each separate shape, in conjunction with the design of the project.

Besides the materials needed for the patches themselves, you will probably find you also need lining material, either for each individual patch as you make it (though this is rarely necessary), or, more commonly, for lining the completed patchwork article. The material used depends entirely on the article. For lining each individual patch a good stiff calico is usually the answer; for lining the entire article the material can vary from ordinary dress lining, if you are making a long patchwork evening skirt, to sheepskin, to line a child's patchwork coat or a jacket for yourself.

Equipment

You will need:

1. Materials (see page 8).

2. Needle, thread, pins and scissors. The needle should not be too coarse for most projects. The colour, strength and consistency of the thread should match the material being used though ordinary sewing cotton is suitable for most materials. Dressmaker's scissors and pins are entirely satisfactory for cutting and pinning together seams and patches.

3. Templates. These provide the 'master shape' — whatever it may be — from which the material is cut out for traditional patchwork designs. You will require both 'solid' templates, which represent the exact shape you desire and are used for cutting round the pattern from which the material is cut, and 'window' templates, which consist of pieces of metal out of which the shape has been cut, so that you can see the shape as if through a window. The latter are used for placing over pieces of material to experiment with pattern and colour before embarking on the actual cutting. Metal templates can be obtained from most large needlework shops. If you have any difficulty in obtaining them, The Needlewoman Shop, 146–48 Regent Street, London W1R 6BA, will supply you with a large range of templates in different shapes and sizes.

Alternatively, you can use pieces of stiff cardboard or some similar material as a substitute for the metal template. For this you will have to draw the required shape yourself (see page 12 for hints on how to do this). The disadvantage of cardboard, of course, is that it will not last indefinitely and you will have to replenish your stock of 'master' shapes from time to time. It is also not as firm as metal.

4. Paper for making temporary linings for each patch. Any paper will do — the stronger and more pliable the better, though it need not be as thick as the substitute card template. It should also be fairly large, because the traditional cutting out technique demands that each patch be cut and pinned or tacked on to an individual paper pattern cut to the right size by folding the paper as shown on page 12 and cutting out several temporary 'linings' from the template.

5. A good working surface, preferably one in which pins and needles can be stuck though this is not essential. Failing all else, use the floor, which at least gives you plenty of space for working on — and the more of this you have the better.

press the
hem allowance
around the cardboard
pattern

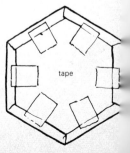

tape

The Basic Method, Using the Hexagon

The most traditional patchwork shape is the hexagon, which consists of six equilateral triangles. It can be copied, if necessary enlarged, from the diagrams illustrated right, that is, if you are using the substitute rather than the prefabricated metal template described in the section on materials and equipment. Once you have your template to hand, cut out several pieces of paper to the exact shape of the template (this can be speeded up by using large pieces of paper, folding each to make several thicknesses and cutting through as many thicknesses as your scissors will allow at the same time). The number of paper 'patterns' needed will depend on the project you have in mind: for most hexagonal projects you will need one for each patch used.

Once you have made a good number of paper patterns, cut out the material itself around the pattern, allowing a bare ½ inch all around (sometimes more or less, depending on how easily the material frays) for seams. If you are using patterned material, remember to make sure you are cutting the exact piece of pattern

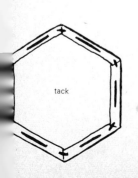

tack

sew one stitch
in each corner

two patches being
oversewn together
from the back

needed for your design (see illustration on page 17). Be sure, for example, that stripes are evenly placed and flowers or particular motifs arc set in the middle of the hexagon (the 'window' template, see page 11, will help you with this). Also, for perfection, be sure that *all* patches are cut so that they can be sewn together with the weave running in the same direction all through the composition — just as though the material had not been cut into patches. This is particularly important for quilts and similar practical patchwork compositions which are easily pulled out of shape. Once all the patches have been cut out — or a section of them if your project is a large one — fold the seams over each paper pattern and either tape or tack (or pin if you are skilled enough to rely on this method) them to the paper as shown in the diagrams on pages 12 and 13. Press each pattern with an iron and either remove the paper pattern there and then or leave it until all sides of the hexagon have been oversewn (this may not be until you have made and collected all the patches needed for your project; again, it depends on the size and nature of the project). It is a good idea to make a separate stitch at each corner (see diagram on page 13) and leave this until the project is finished to keep the edges of material in place, for example, when washing and ironing. The paper pattern, if left, also provides a support during the oversewing.

Oversewing to join the patches together (as demonstrated in the right hand diagram on page 13) is nearly always done by hand owing to the complexity of the figure (only very large hexagons are worth machining), but this makes a relaxed and pleasant task and although it takes a comparatively long time, the finished result is always excellent. Once all the patches have been joined together, the article is edged, lined, if the project calls for it, and finally washed and ironed or dry cleaned.

This is the basic patchwork technique and is followed, in one way or another, for all traditional patchwork projects. Obviously there is more to patchwork than this and each project demands different subsidiary techniques, details and other considerations not yet discussed, but once you have grasped the basic principle, you are ready to begin.

Designs based on the hexagon

If the most traditional patchwork shape is the hexagon, the most traditional hexagonal design is the 'star' or 'flower' made up of seven hexagons as shown in the diagrams opposite. The 'flowers' or 'stars' can be built up using a variety of patterns and contrasting colours to make each one attractive. A similarly patterned centre patch (see illustration on page 9) in each flower helps to make the individual flower more distinct.

If you are using this flower shape in an article, do not attempt to collect all the hexagons for your project and then join them all together. It is far easier to join your individual hexagons into flower shapes first, and then continue to join these together. This method also allows experiment with the design: if you are not working to an already carefully thought out plan, you can

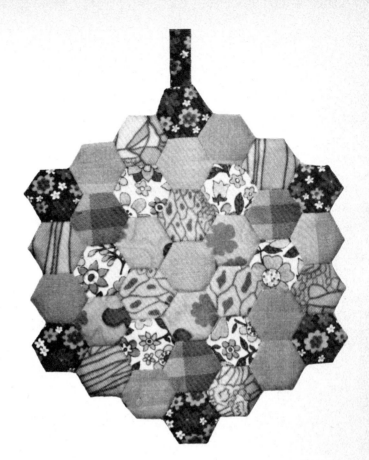

...t-holder in plain and ...tterned hexagons: darker ...tches mark the corners; ...e lining is in a plain colour, ...e interlining is of plastic ...am.

shuffle the flowers around until you arrive at a pleasing combination. Notice, for example, how the flowers on the skirt illustrated on page 9 grow darker towards the hem, making a pleasing effect. Another way of using colour in a design is to move from, for example, green through blue to violet. This is a technique much used in painting. Whatever you do, work by daylight if colour plays a large part in your design: certain colours can look quite different under electric lighting.

...ditional hexagon designs.

A skirt sewn in two matchir
widths with seam at the
sides.
The lengths are reversed for
the zip fastener to be sewn *
The sides of each hexagon
are $2\frac{1}{4}$ inches long without
seam allowance.

Hexagonal flowers against a background

Once all the necessary hexagonal flowers for your project have
been made (by oversewing each of the seven individual
hexagons together — see page 13), you can either simply join
the flowers together, as in the skirt on page 9, or place them
against a background, as in the bedspread on page 9. If the
flowers are highly patterned, make the background quiet and
uniform unless you have some unusual, brilliant contrast in
mind. Another way of showing up the flowers is to make the
background patches in the same pattern but to a smaller scale:
the flowers will then stand out as if they were comparatively
large against the small patterned background. Or again, for
large surfaces such as quilts you can make the flowers themselves form the pattern against a plain patchwork background;
for example, they could be arranged in garlands or criss-crosses.

The skirt can also be stitche
so that the hexagons fit
together all round, but this
more difficult.

*ined and padded rocking-
*air cover made of large,
*ght 'flower' shapes on a
*ackground of hexagons cut
*om a material patterned
*ith small flowers so that
*e background pattern
*ows off the main one.
*he cover is finished with
*arrow edging. The pattern
*used may suggest ideas
r quilts and cushions.

Patchwork rug using hexagons

Patches forming a 'mosaic' pattern can be used as the basis for
a rug or something similar. If you cut patches into points as
shown in the diagram top right on page 18 and sew them into
the seams between the rows of hexagons, you will end up
with a result something like the edge of the flower illustrated on
page 18. This idea can be amplified not only to make rugs,
but also for edging cushions or decorations or for throwing
details of a pattern into relief. An attractive effect can be
achieved by mixing ordinary hexagonal patches with the
occasional loose piece cut into points.

17

The same technique can be used with a background of squares or triangles, though of course the effect will be somewhat different. The pointed pieces may also vary in shape. You can make them long or short or lobate in many different ways. Again, as for ordinary patchwork, do not use material which frays easily — the effect might be charming at the outset, but your work would quickly fall apart.

A variation on the patchwork rug theme is the 'rag-rug', a technique which entails machine-stitching row after row of torn strips (about 5–6 inches long) laid flat. The strips are attached to a firm foundation (jute is a good material to use) and when one row has been sewn on, it is turned in at the side to form an edge and the next row is then sewn on about half an inch or less away from the previous row. This process is continued until the whole surface is covered with strips and the foundation no longer visible.

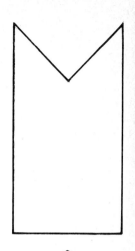

Detail of sunflower shows how each hexagon is stitched with 'petal' patches.

The pattern shapes for sunflowers shown in full scale without seam allowance

The thicker lines show where the 'petal' patches are stitch in between the rows of hexa

...he completed flower.

Flowers

The same technique can be used for edging hexagonal 'flowers'. The hexagons in the inside section of the sunflower illustrated above are in a brown material interwoven with gold threads. At the edge are three rows of yellow hexagons covered with pieces of corduroy in the same colour which have been cut into points and attached to the seams of the rug. If you give the flower a good backing and pad it well with horse hair, foam rubber or some other suitable padding material, it could make a most attractive cushion. Or you could pad the centre only, stretching the rest into a curve of some kind to make a wall decoration. This small flower is intended as an inspiration or starting point for your own ideas on the 'rug' theme.

Pentagons

Following the basic method, pentagons (that is, five-sided shapes, see diagrams right) can be used in patchwork to make a whole variety of everyday objects just that little bit different — even for patchwork. Pentagonal shapes sewn together automatically curve to make spheres or 'bodies'. These geometrical 'bodies' can be made into balls, cushions, pin-cushions, and so on. Stuff them with rags, sand, pieces of foam rubber or some such suitable material before sewing in the final patch. Alternatively, a ball, for example, can be left hollow (this will make it lighter and therefore more suitable for very young children) in which case a sturdy pliable stiffening must be used to back the article (Vilene is excellent). Pentagonal boxes can be made on the same principle, joining one side of one patch on one side only or leaving the patch completely separate to serve as a 'lid'. Thin silk patches lined with a transparent non-inflammable material make beautiful translucent lamp-shades; stiffened with wire, they will make complete modern-looking lamps to stand on a flat surface (make sure the wire is well covered to avoid scratches). Fold the corners of one pentagonal patch over, as demonstrated in the middle diagram right, and you have a Christmas 'star' to tie on the window; eleven such 'stars' joined together will make a lantern. Small tablecloths or place mats can be very quickly made in the same way as the Christmas 'star': Cut the smaller pentagon (see middle diagram right) out of different material and stitch down the corners following one of the methods described in the section on appliqué work (page 64).

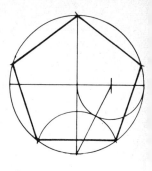

Small cushions which look like orange segments.

1 ◠ 1 ◯

The ball (opposite) is sewn semi-circles folded in the middle and tapering patches as shown in the diagrams (right). The segments are fastened at each corner.

12 ◠ 12 ◠

Small cushions and a special ball

The 'orange segments' shown in the illustration opposite were originally intended to be sewn together into a large ball, but they could equally well be used as cushions — they make particularly comfortable car cushions. Each 'segment' is composed of a circular patch folded down the centre and stitched together with a 'shell' shape (this 'shell' or 'clam' shape is available as a template), leaving a small opening for the stuffing before completing the stitching.

Instead of making a solid ball out of 'segments' you can also make a special, easy-to-hold ball for a small baby as shown in the illustration below. The principle used for making the 'segments' for the ball is the same, only a semicircular piece of material is substituted for the circular piece, as demonstrated in the diagrams at left bottom. Once the segments have been made and stuffed, join them all at the corners as illustrated. For this ball you will need twelve segments.

The diagrams below show just five of the many 'bodies' that can be made out of the regular shapes described in this book, and the number and shape of patches needed for each one:

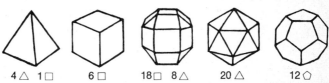

4 △ 1 □   6 □   18 □ 8 △   20 △   12 ⬠

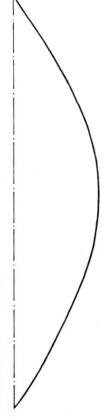

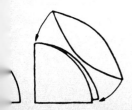

...is ball can be made larger ...smaller than the one ...own. If it is made to the ...ggested size it will be just ...ht for a baby to hold.

Quadrangles

The square is the simplest of the regular shapes to use in patchwork and it is a good one for the beginner to start on. While it
has not the scope or the intriguing beauty of the hexagon, the
square nevertheless lends itself to many uses in patchwork.
A big point in its favour, particularly for the beginner who
wants to experiment without spending too much time, is that
the square is infinitely quicker to join up than any other shape.
Whole rows of squares can be simply placed in the right order
and machined into panels which can then easily be joined
together.

To start, cut out each square as described in the section
headed 'The Basic Method' following the weave of the thread.
Arrange them side by side in a simple pattern, for example,
one light, one dark, or in stripes, or zigzags, or if you want to

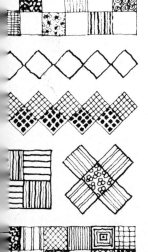

wing machine cover of uare patches sewn gether, in an irregular but ll-balanced arrangement.

be a bit more adventurous, place whole surfaces, borders or check patterns against a plain background or collect strong coloured squares and place them in eye-catching array against a dull neutral background. Alternatively, try arranging light and dark, patterned and unpatterned patches to form as even a surface as possible. That is how the squares in the sewing machine cover illustrated above have been arranged. Such arranging is a simple and pleasant exercise in the composition of patterns. If you feel like experimenting before embarking on your project in material, cut out light and dark or patterned paper squares and use them to shuffle round until you arrive at a pleasing pattern. Such paper squares can easily be made using graph paper and a child's box of crayons.

As a rule, the actual articles made from square patches are rectangular and it is therefore easy to calculate the number of squares needed. However if you intend to sew a strip of uniform width round the side of your article, you must remember to take all such edging into account when calculating the size of your checks.

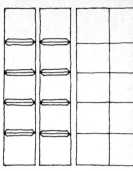

Lengths of matching panels.

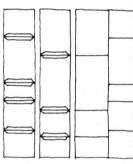

Lengths of unmatched panels.

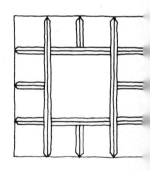

Square panels.

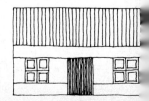

Design using panels.

Joining quadrilateral patches together

The simplest method of sewing quadrilateral patches together is to machine them first into lengths as indicated in the first paragraph, then press the seams flat with an iron, tack or pin the lengths together crosswise and stitch or machine them together into a single surface. To make sure the different patches match exactly once they have been machined into lengths, be extra careful to measure and cut out accurately in the first place: the square is such a simple shape it is tempting to be slapdash about cutting out, and this can make for disappointing results.

Certain patterns, for example, those requiring different sized rectangles rather than simple squares, are best stitched into units rather than lengths before the final sewing is undertaken. The detail illustrated above, for example, is from a cot cover in which the rectangles in each 'length' are of many different proportions. For this the rectangles were first sewn into units regardless of the joins between each 'panel'. It is, however, sometimes difficult to apportion coloured and patterned panels on an irregular design and in such cases stitching lengthwise sometimes helps; also, if the project is to be lined, it is best to machine through some of the lengthwise seams to hold the patchwork, lining and any interlining together.

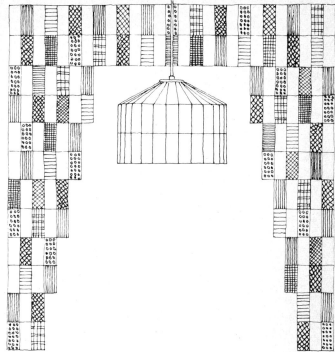

*...uggestions for,
...bove, a kitchen curtain
...nd a lampshade;
...elow, pot-holder.
...he panels are evenly
...istributed according to
...olour and pattern.*

Curtains and blinds using rectangles

Square patchwork makes most effective curtains and window blinds. Choose either closely woven material and line it so that the seams do not show on the outside, or else a thin transparent material, in which case use a thin lining. Thin white string woven into patches and lace are also effective. If all this sounds too complicated and time-consuming, try making curtains or blinds out of completely identical plain patches — this too can be very effective if the fabric is well chosen. Instead of lining curtains made of thin material the joins can be made on the 'right' side and covered with narrow ribbon or edging. This makes attractive markings when the work is seen with the light behind it. Monograms and embroidered pieces from worn linen can also be cut out to make decorative patches when 'welded' together with unpatterned patches or panels (page 31 gives several suggestions for the use of patches with monograms).

The illustrations on these pages are designed to give you some idea of what can be made of square patchwork and inspire you to start sewing. The possibilities are endless, even using just rectangles, and once you start, you will find your own ideas taking shape and your interest in different aspects of the craft developing.

Wall decoration in a combination of the techniques described on this page. Note the attractive variations in colour, colour depth and division of surface. Don't worry if the patches are uneven in width or length: simply join them up and turn in the outer edge of the whole design for an even finish. The mixture of velvet, silk, wool, cotton and beads produces a pleasing general impression.

A special patchwork technique

This technique was originally used for making quilts out of silk. The patches used here are not large, indeed, most are only narrow strips. The easiest way to set about a project using this technique is to work with a lining material. This is not absolutely necessary, much depends on the material used: if, for example, you are using silk, lining is vital because silk alone is too brittle; stronger materials which do not fray or pull out of shape may be used without a lining. If you *are* using a lining as advised, sew each panel of material separately on to the square of lining material used.

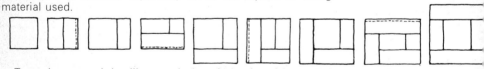

To make a panel (as illustrated above), begin with a small centre panel and sew the patches on in layers until the square or panel has reached the size you desire. Machine-stitch or use small back-stitching to join the patches together and press or tack down the seams on the right side. Every second horizontal diagram illustrated on this page shows how the patches are sewn on; the alternative diagrams show the effect once the patches have been turned down and pressed. The numbered diagrams (right) indicate the order in which each patch has been sewn on. Once made, the panels can be joined together in the ordinary fashion to make window blinds (see illustration opposite), curtains, quilts, mats and so on.

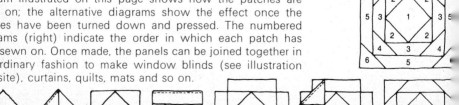

Suggestions for distribution of light and dark patches.

Creating a rectangular design against a background

A large project can be made into a puzzle picture with, for instance, figures in relief on a mass of patches as illustrated in the patchwork quilt above. To create this sort of effect it is a good idea to start by making a small outline sketch which, with the aid of graph paper or a projector, can be enlarged to the actual size of the project. This will serve as a guide or pattern on which patches can be arranged following the paper outline.

28

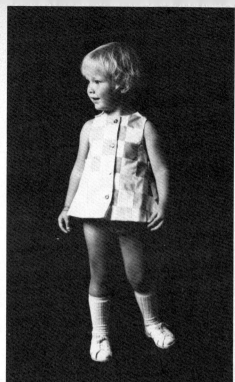

*...med patches make
...rming clothes for children.
...e are two variations of a
...'s frock made from
...ares of cotton material.*

*...the left a large quilt with
...eat variety of patches.
...s makes a pleasing effect.*

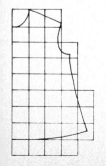

Clothes

If you choose to make a patchwork garment it is because you want something different from the multitude of clothes to be found on most shop rails. Such a garment doesn't take long to make, is relatively cheap and, in this day and age of factory-made uniformity, is completely individual. Charming patchwork garments can also be made for children, and these do not call for so many patches and are even less time-consuming. Patchwork clothes for fancy dress parties or amateur theatricals are other invariably successful projects. More elaborate garments for 'best' or everyday wear are also a possibility — a dress, cape or jacket, perhaps, with bag to match or a pair of patchwork boots.

Another good use for patchwork is if you have a length of material you like very much but haven't enough of to make a whole garment. By using patchwork you can supplement the lack with some suitable material and make a complete garment.

When making patchwork clothes it is important to adjust the size of the pieces to the paper pattern used. Calculate the size from the most important parts of the garment. Then sew the patches together into sections of approximately the right size and cut them round the pattern as normal. If the garment is to be a warm one and not crease too easily, line it and, for warmth, finish with quilting (see page 42).

Accessories

Patches can make delightful bags, belts and ties providing you choose suitable materials such as pieces of discarded sportswear, leather or, if you weave or have a friend who does weaving as a hobby, the small sample pieces and ends of woven stuff. All such toughish materials can be stitched together in a variety of ways to make the most attractive accessories. A tie could be made out of couple of left over pieces from, say, a dress. When making ties, don't be afraid to experiment with patchwork combinations of flowers, dots, stripes or checks. The same applies to caps, and in both cases the results can be delightful.

Patchwork bags can be immensely varied. Small elegant evening bags can be made from left over pieces of new material or scraps embellished with embroidery or monograms. For larger bags try using the ends of trouser legs as your basic material, stitching on a leather base, pockets and side pieces. Chair seats made from patterned leather cut-outs appliquéd on a wool material will stand much wear and tear. Shoe and slipper bags can be made from odds and ends — not to mention the slippers themselves. Practical storage pockets for the car or cloakroom — indeed, almost anything — can be made from patches with a little imagination!

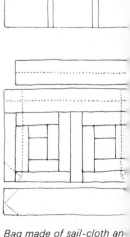

Bag made of sail-cloth an
other patches in similarly
strong material. Each side
consists of two panels, bo
made following the techni
described on page 24; all
four panels have patches
the same pattern. The wh
effect is varied but discipli

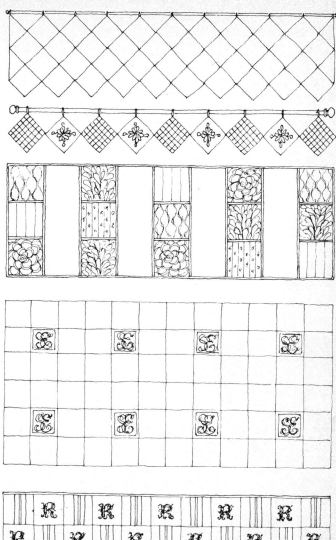

*Suggestions for pelmets in panels joined vertically or diagonally,
corner to corner. The diagram second from top has panels sewn on the
back, fastened diagonally at the corners and hung on rings.
Draperies can be sewn in a similar way.
The two bottom diagrams show panels with monograms from towels
or table napkins, suitable for use as decoration for window blinds
and curtains.*

Tablecloths

Patchwork tablecloths present endless scope for the imagination. They can, for example, be made up entirely of patches or perhaps just partly of patches; they can be in colour and patterned or simply white. One good idea is to save the best pieces of worn handwoven tablecloths and napkins and make them into patches to be stitched together as patchwork tablecloths, using ribbon or decorative stitching to hide the joins. If your old tablecloths had monograms or embroidery, cut them out as well, with just enough material around each to make a simple shape, preferably a square. These can be stitched together to make a pretty centre piece, to appliqué on to a suitable base, or to join up with other patches. They can also be used for the festive table decoration. If the patchwork made from the materials suggested results in a somewhat delicate cloth, use it for special occasions only — it's fun, for instance, to have a special birthday cloth — perhaps presented in the first place as a special birthday gift.

Both rectangular and round tablecloths can be given an overhanging edge of square patches to keep your cloth in place. Calculate the patch measurements according to the sides or circumference of your table. This is an especially good plan for use out-of-doors as the wind often makes it difficult to keep an ordinary cloth in place.

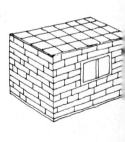

Creating a 'play tent' over a table

Making a 'play tent' over a table can keep the whole family busy. First of all a sketch must be made, measuring length, width and height of table, not forgetting to take the 'door' and 'window' into account in your calculations. Perhaps father is the best person for this task. Meanwhile, everyone can collect large and small patches and then help put them together. In the general enthusiasm do not forget that the size must be correct and all measurements must tally with those on the sketch plan if the result is to be successful. Machining will join the patches quickly and well. If you are planning to make an extremely fine, beautifully made tent, it must also have an inside lining with patches to represent, for example, the kitchen and kitchen equipment.

There are various ways of tackling the tent 'door'. Just an opening or a piece of material hanging down will suffice, but if

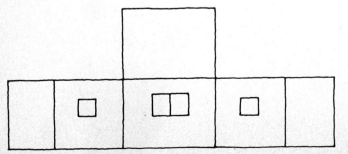

you happen to have a large old zip handy, this will make a much more satisfying job. To make a window, cut out a piece of tent to the shape and height required and edge it with a strong strip of material. If necessary, stitch one or two strips across the window for support. The window will look even cosier if you add a curtain — simply stitch a piece of transparent material to the inside, or, even better, thread the 'curtain' through a piece of string or wire and attach this to the tent so that the 'curtain' may be pulled back when desired.

If the window is made large enough, it can double as a 'theatre' for a puppet show. Add a patch to the outside stitched only at the top to act as a curtain which can be rolled up and fastened with a button or nylon strip while the performance is taking place. Alternatively, you could hang the 'curtain' from rings on a cord. Patches will also provide the puppets and their clothes, of course (see page 70-1).

ove, a table 'tent'. Right,
gestions for hand puppets,
n out of mittens. The
g's head is more mobile
n those of the others.
ts into the mitten's seam
d has a hole for one finger
manipulate it.

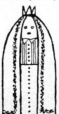

Using large rectangles

On a large surface large squares can be moved around until a design is worked out. The starting point could be a representational picture of, for example, a building or some such suitable subject which calls mainly for rectangular patches. Do not forget that the colours you choose will play an important part in creating not only atmosphere, but also certain effects in your pictures. For example, bold bright colours will stand out and give an impression of nearness; misty blues and greys will recede to create the impression of a background.

*eft. A composition in which
he individual's imagination is
iven free play around
istinguishable buildings.
he five light squares could
epresent stars, and at the
ottom the contrasting
atches may represent water
r perhaps a flight of steps.*

*ight. A wall hanging with a
onspicuous design. The
ouses have a quiet
ackground in a light grey
ne and the whole surface of
e design is well-balanced.*

Triangles and Rhomboids

There are two varieties of triangle used in patchwork: one is equilateral, that is, it has equal sides and therefore equal angles (see diagram 1); the other has one angle of 90°, that is, half a rectangle divided diagonally (see diagram 2). Both types of triangle are easy to work with and can combine to form the most beautiful mosaic patterns. These do not have to be complex: some of the most effective mosaic patterns are created by simple combinations of stripes and checks, dark and light colours or plain and patterned materials (see diagrams below). A bedspread or a round tablecloth, for example, could consist of just one large star made up of suitably contrasting triangular patches.

Both triangles are easily drawn and cut out (for readers who are not using templates) — either by using a set square or, for an equilateral triangle, by dividing a hexagon into six, and for a triangle with one angle of 90°, by dividing any rectangle in half diagonally (see diagrams below and right).

The triangles described also form the basis of two diamond-shaped rhomboids (that is, figures in which only the *opposite* sides and angles are equal (see diagrams 3 and 4). When making a design using either triangles or rhomboids it is particularly important to tack or tape them first over cardboard patterns (see page 12) before joining together because these figures are particularly prone to stretching out of shape. For some designs it is possible to machine these shapes together but usually hand stitching is necessary.

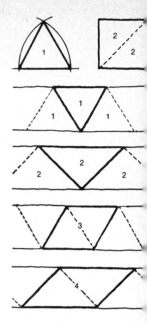

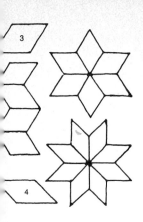

3

4

*ove. Two forms of
*mboid which, owing to
*eir different angles, can be
*ade into entirely different
r shapes.

*ght. Detail of an American
*tchwork quilt with bunches
*f flowers in large and small
uares.

5

5

*ove. Two more types of
*mboid (5); above right,
w they may be combined.

*ht. These two types of
*mboid machine - stitched
ether.

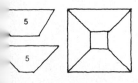

Transparent mosaic patterned patchwork

Transparent coloured triangular or rhomboidal patches can be combined together in pretty patterns to make stars, lampshades and window blinds which give the effect of leaded window panes. The prettiest colour combinations are undoubtedly to be obtained using a very thin silk but if colour does not fit in with your existing room scheme (and it is best to be sparing with mosaic or motley patterns in interior decorating schemes), then try using white lace or net, which will give a most subtle effect of contrasting texture and detail (for more about curtains and window blinds see page 25).

Whichever material you choose, once all or a section of patches have been made (depending on how large the project is to be) lay them in the proposed design on a transparent foundation (any thin lining material will do) which has been stretched over a wooden or metal frame (make sure the design allows space for this). If you do not possess a frame specially designed for patchwork, use a large ordinary needlework or tapestry frame. Then join the patches together as described on page 13, attaching them at intervals to the lining. For a particularly neat finish cover the joins with an embroidery stitch (see page 74), or with a narrow ribbon or edging sewn on with tiny 'invisible' stitches from the back. This finish will also help keep the finished design in shape.

The diagrams opposite give ideas for mosaic patterns using rectangles and triangles. Each pattern has tension points which are indicated by the marks at the edge of each diagram.

How to make a mosaic pattern stand out

By judicious use of light, dark and striped patches a pattern can be made to look as though it were depicted in relief (see left and centre diagrams below). A sense of perspective can also be achieved by careful juxtaposition of different shapes (see diagram right). Triangles and rhomboids are the easiest shapes with which to create such effects.

'Reflections' can be made by inserting patches made from materials with reflective qualities such as certain plasticised fabrics, moiré and ordinary silk. Alternatively, turn this theme the other way round, as it were, and paste ordinary cloth patches around the edge of a mirror.

The patterns illustrated right are intended to inspire ideas for methodical patchwork designs. Make a sketch of the lines shown and try to produce a variety of effects. This is an interesting exercise which can lead to many variations.

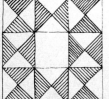
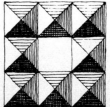
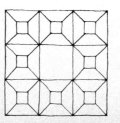

Left. Suggestions for mirror frames made from patches sewn together. The middle diagram shows how four different coloured fabrics may form trompe l'oeil pyramid effects.

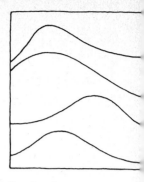

Draw the pattern on paper.

Irregular Shapes

Even irregular shapes can be joined together and used for special effects in patchwork, although it would be unwise for the beginner to start with these, however unusual and exciting the result, because unforeseen problems can occur. A simple method of experimenting with irregular shapes is to use a good lining material as a base and simply sew on one patch after another, regardless of size or shape, fitting them in as you go, rather like making a crazy paving. This can make most effective quilts, draperies, and bedspreads, not to mention artistic wall decorations. Either begin with a design in mind and hunt out the necessary patches, or start with the pieces of material you have to hand and weld them into some sort of pattern. The shapes themselves can be large or small, circular or angular, strips, zigzags, amorphous squiggles — the variety is endless and the practice particularly satisfying — or challenging — to those who feel hampered — or easily bored — by the more conventional shapes.

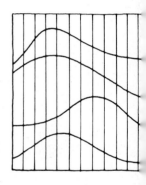

Cut the pattern into strips.

If you are planning a large project, mark out the overall measurements and perhaps even draw a design on a sheet of lining material. If you intend to hang your piece of work, make absolutely sure the thread or weave is running the same way on all the patches (it should be anyway) and that the materials used are of practically identical thickness. Do not forget to allow for seams when you cut around the edges of your patches, just as you would for a regular-shaped patch. Once all patches are cut out, stitch the seams together either by hand or machine and line the work, again, just as you would for a regular-shaped patch design.

The curtain illustrated right was made from irregularly shaped patches sewn into strips. It could just have easily been made up from continuous pieces of material, but the strips were in fact part of the design and had the added advantage of making it possible to make a large project from comparatively small patches. Remember, if you are inspired to make something like this, to allow for the seams not only of the individual patches but also of the strips, and in such a way that the curved lines of this pattern, for example, continue without a break from strip to strip.

Right. Curtain made of plai
checked and striped materi
sewn in strips.

40

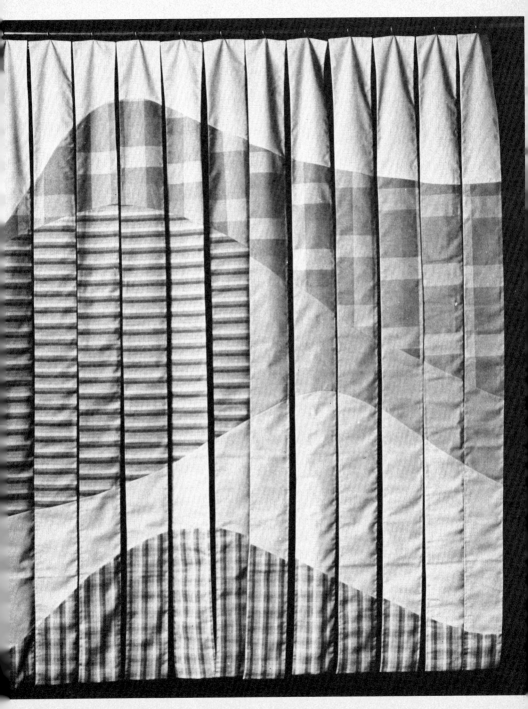

41

Quilting

Quilting is an old technique, designed to hold together lining, wadding and outer material, which has long been used in Europe and America particularly for clothes and bed quilts. A wadded quilted cover is warm and pretty and need not be ironed. The technique is often used for work in seamed patches and appliqué. In the latter case quilting can be used to hold, for example, a heavy appliqué embroidery on a firm lining material.

The most usual material for quilting is a complete interlining of a porous material, but a loose yarn, threaded with a coarse needle in between rows of quilting, can also be used. Most quilting can be done by machine or by hand.

The best results are obtained if you work with some kind of frame. If you are machine sewing then careful tacking must be undertaken instead. Large articles *must* be handsewn, unless they can be made in small sections which are then stitched together. Large quilt frames are available, constructed rather like looms, with bars for rolling up the quilt. Simple frames can also be constructed at home from wooden laths. When finished, these will look and operate rather like a needlework frame, with holes bored through the laths and pegs to fix your position. Clamps can also be used for stretching. In fact, large projects can be sewn and quilted in sections in an ordinary needlework frame and then sewn together. This is often a more convenient way of setting about your project, as in small modern flats it is often difficult to make room for a real quilt frame. Also the work inevitably takes a long time and the frame has to stand about as long as the work remains unfinished. For speed, and enjoyment as well, why not organise a combined effort, with several people working on the same project at once? This method of cooperation is often used by charities, who then sell their handiwork.

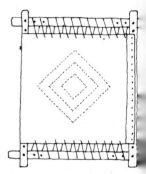

Above. Needlework frame with binding nailed on to hold the work firm.

Above. If you haven't a quilting frame make one from wooden laths.

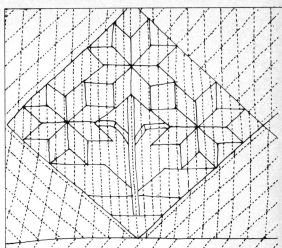

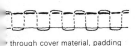

through cover material, padding

lining in the seams between
hes.

hes appliquéd in rounds following

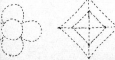

n patterns.

Whether you work on a frame or not, the method of quilting itself is the same. The only substantial difference is that on a frame the lining material is stretched as evenly as possible and the finished result is therefore neater. However, satisfactory results can be obtained by smoothing the work out on a table, for example, or on some such large flat working surface. Another method frequently used for large projects is to do the actual patchwork parts of the work on your knees. Lining and interlining are stretched or spread out together with the top cover. The interlining may be quilt wadding, washed wool, felt, flannel, terry or some synthetic material — indeed, whatever is suitable for your purpose, but whatever you use make sure it really is suitable, and that it doesn't shrink, for example, if you intend to wash the completed article. Unless they are stretched on a frame, remember to tack the different layers accurately together in several places. For the actual quilting process either follow the seams between the patches of the pattern of the material, or alternatively work from lines drawn in chalk. These can be made with a ruler or with circular cut-out patterns, either before or after the stretching.

Handsewn quilting generally calls for small backstitching. If you are using wadding or some other thick material, the needle should be thin with a small eye and should be pointed as straight up or down as possible. Place one hand under the work and the other over to steady it. If the layers of stuff to be sewn together are thin enough, you may find it possible to sew from the top and take several stitches on the needle at once. Use special quilting thread (this can be bought at good needle-work shops) or very strong thread. In order to hide the fastening-off, tuck all thread ends and knots into the interlining. To give a good 'finish' to your work, add a strip of ribbon or some suitable material.

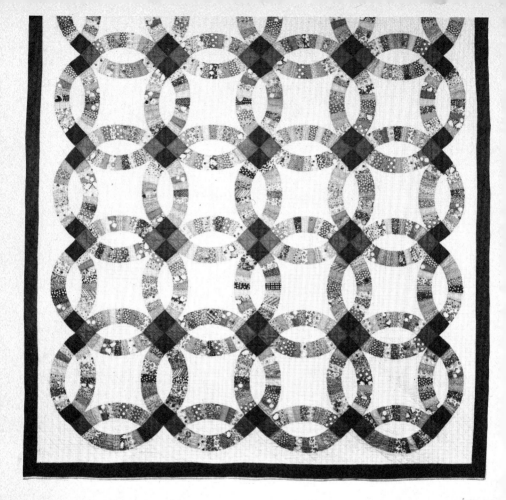

American patchwork quilting

Of all patchwork articles, the most traditional and the one which probably springs first to mind at the mention of 'patchwork', is the American patchwork quilt, an article which has long been used and esteemed in America. The technique was probably introduced by European immigrants and used at first as a matter of necessity; whatever, the quilt was swiftly re-exported and taken up with enthusiasm by European needlewomen.

Many of the designs are traditional, handed down from generation to generation. Above is an example of a well-designed, well-sewn quilt with a design of large intertwining rings and a wealth of detail in the small patterned cotton patches. The squares in the quilt (see detail illustrated opposite) are in pink, the border in a delicate blue and the background white. A detail from another American quilt is shown on page 37. Both quilts use a combination of pure patchwork and appliqué. Both,

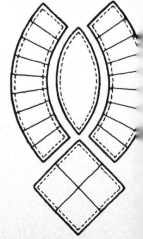

Above. Detail of an American
patchwork quilt.
Complete view of the
pattern.

like most American quilts, are also closely and well quilted, which strengthens the seams and accounts to a large extent for their hard-wearing qualities.

The curved parts of the rings in the illustration above are composed of small patches stitched together on the wrong side with small backstitches. The slightly larger square patches were sewn together into bands in the same way. When carrying out this sort of work it is most helpful to draw the pattern on to a thin lining material first and tack down the seamed patches as soon as each one is ready. The white background patches of the above quilt were cut out with a generous allowance for seams and appliquéd on last with invisible stitches to cover the raw edges of the patterned patches. To soften the very angular corners the process was reversed at the corners and the juxtaposed material turned in and appliquéd instead. Quilting followed the shape of the patches except, of course, where these were sewn into panels first to make a foundation.

Detail which shows how effective frayed strips of material tacked together can be.

'Painting' with Patches

Just as a design is reproduced in painting, so too can it be made with patches, and many people who would not dream of painting can give expression to their creative talents by just sticking or stitching patches on to a foundation. You can either shape and arrange the patches according to traditional patterns or, using your imagination, move them around to create your own design. An apparently casual and almost careless work often has freshness and charm; careful execution on the other hand, also has its merits. Amateurs, just like professional artists, have their own personal modes of expression.

Collage implies designs using paper and glue but the same technique can also be used for applying the material to the foundation. A textile glue is obviously best, but there is also a spray paste and paste in sheet form on the market, both of which are perfectly satisfactory. The latter is pressed on with an iron and is particularly useful.

Appliqué is the equivalent of collage for material and involves machining or handsewing patches on to a foundation.

'Fun' designs

With imagination and lots of patches both children and grown-ups can make most amusing designs, working alone or as part of a 'team'. Collage and appliqué offer the most unexpected possibilities and the finished result may be purely decorative or have a practical function as well.

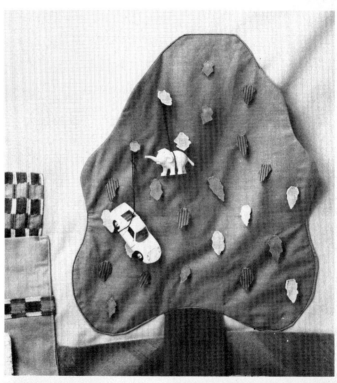

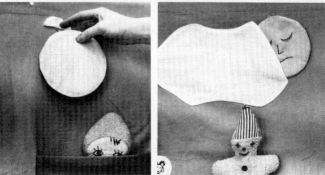

...t. Details of the nursery
... hanging shown in
...ur on page 79.
...sun is a yellow circle
... heliotrope lining — the
...n. It can be removed
... a hook under the cloud
... made to creep in under
...loud. This hanging has
... pockets with individual
...ls appliquéd on to the
...rials.

Naturalistic designs

These are designs which reproduce objects in a life-like manner, for example from an illustration or a colour slide. If you are planning to work on a large scale, it is most helpful to project the picture on to a large sheet of paper (as already described on page 28) and draw in the most important outlines before embarking on the actual project. Choice of material and method depend not only on the appearance of the design, but also on where and how the decoration (if it is to be a decoration) is to hang (see page 62 on mounting and hanging). Curtains and draperies usually have a stylized type of decoration, but may also have very naturalistic designs. The illustration opposite, for example, shows a tree on which grouse are displaying their feathers. The foundation material is a thin blue-grey linen which gives an impression of open space. The tree and the birds are pictured in true-to-life colours, in patches of material which have been pasted on, partly overlapping one another. The completed design has been sewn to the foundation using zig-zag stitches and, with the light behind it, stands out as a dark silhouette. With the light in front changes of colour and lustre in the patches of material produce quite a different effect, just as it would naturally.

Stylized designs

Popular choices for appliqué designs are houses, plants, animals and people, all of which lend themselves to a formal, stylized treatment just as well as to a simple and naturalistic, naive or constructive treatment. Stylization gives more scope for experiment for example in space, light and harmony. Closely related colour tones can be employed to give the design perspective. If you haven't the patches to obtain a desired colour gradation, cut up a piece of worn material into patches and dye these, using cold water dye, to suit your design or scale of colours.

Don't be afraid to mix techniques. In a stylized design there may well be a good reason for sewing certain pieces of your design together and pasting others on. You may need to cut away parts of certain patches in order to show up the background. Windows, doors and arches can easily be conjured up by judicious cutting, and the technique is equally suitable for other uses (see sewn and described models on pages 90 and 92).

Luckily wall decorations need not be washed very often so you can usually get away with partly pasting and partly sewing. If your creation is really delicate, however, cover it with glass, rather than run the risk of ruining it by ordinary cleaning methods.

ght. A large composition
hose huge pointing spires
ggest infinity. It can easily
imagined in various
ades and materials,
rticularly wool, cotton,
en, silk and velvet.
ft. Detail.

Methods, focal points and details

One of the principal artistic rules which holds goods for patch-work just as much as for painting is that every composition must have a main focal point which first catches the eye when the work is viewed at a distance. Detail is for closer inspection, to keep the interest alive and provide a background which does not 'fight' with the main focal point. Details also help to clarify the impression to be conveyed to the spectator. The illustration opposite of a man lying on the grass demonstrates both the main focal point and the function of detail. The aim of the composition is to convey how pleasant it is to lie on the grass.

Begin with the main focal point on the figure. This must be large, and drawn perhaps with the help of squared paper as demonstrated below. Paste or sew it on in a suitable position leaving the contours unsewn so that the flowers and leaves can be stitched in and around the figure. Cut out the sun and birds and place them in position. Then cut as many flowers and leaves as you please and fix them on at random round the figure. At the front let them reach almost halfway up the body, at the back partly tuck them under the figure so that a really vivid impression is created of flowers surrounding the man.

Enlarging designs with the help of squared paper

A small sketch can be enlarged with the help of squared paper. First rule a network of small squares over the design to be enlarged, then rule large squares on a sheet of paper the desired size, making sure that both sets of squares are in pro-portion — that is, that you have the same *number* of squares and the same proportion between height and width. It is then relatively easy to enlarge the outline of the large figure using intersection points between squares as a guide.

Right. A large wall hanging which can be sewn or pasted. The shoes are made of suede, the rest of the decoration is made of felt and cotton material.

Below. Enlarge the outlines of the figure by using squared paper as instructed.

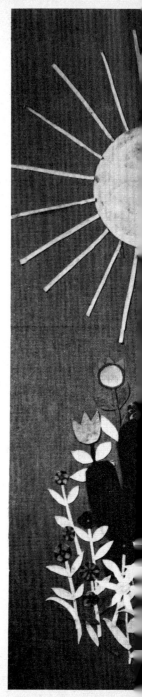

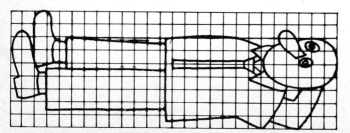

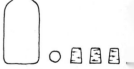

Left. Flower and bud made up of circles cut from plain and patterned cotton mater The petals are spread out and fastened with a pleat at one end.

Left. A patchwork pig suitable for children to ma from a bottle on four cork. The body is decorated wit yellow, red and pink cotto squares pasted all over the surface; the ears and tail a stitched at one end only. Use a cork or ball for the snout.

Designs using patches of uniform shape

Hundreds of designs or parts of designs can ·be built up in a
life-like manner from uniformly shaped, partially overlapping
patches. Using this technique you can make, for example,
fishes with scales, birds with feathers, flowers with petals,
tree-tops with foliage. First mark out the outside shape then
arrange the patches according to a definite system. Flowers,
for example, are best begun from the centre or the outside edge;
fishes or birds from one end. The same principle can be used
on patchwork quilts, to sew on irregularly cut patches by
machine.

Another technique is to scatter patches over a surface so that
they cover one another in irregular formation like leaves on the
ground. If you do this, however, take care to vary dark and light,
patterned and plain patches and to fasten each patch provision-
ally where it falls with pins or tape.

How to avoid frayed edges

Some materials fray more than others. Leather, felt and cloth do not fray at all; all woven materials fray to some extent. There are various ways of avoiding or minimizing fraying. One way is to press adhesive material firmly on to the wrong side of the material before cutting it out. Another, very laborious way is to machine stitch a seam right round the inside of the drawn outline. The illustration on this page shows how fraying can be avoided by cutting patches with pinking shears; this is obviously the quickest method and the serrated edges may even contribute to the effect of the pattern. For some projects it is a good idea to cut the patches double and sew them together on the wrong side. Of course, you can always treat the patches very carefully and stitch them on as soon as they are cut out!

Making a large design from small patches

A simple way of achieving this is to begin by cutting out the desired large size on a sheet of adhesive paper. Then stick small patch after small patch on to the paper and finally trim the outline with scissors. With the aid of a duplicate adhesive sheet you can then press the design firmly on to a backing. Naturally the design can be stitched instead of stuck on.

'Feather' patches

To make birds' feathers (see also page 49), lay patches one by

On large patches jagged edges are hardly noticeable, they show up best against a contrasting background. Note (left) the order in which the patches overlap.

one over the whole surface to be covered, beginning at the neck and working systematically downwards overlapping each patch with the next. In the above illustration the 'feathers' have been cut out with pinking shears to give a ruffled effect, but you can equally well make them smooth. If all patches used are of the same shape, the finished outline will be uneven; in the illustration the outer patches have been turned in to make the outline even: either procedure is effective.

On the birds in the illustration you will notice how the variation between dark and light patches has been skilfully arranged to emphasize the weighty character of their bodies. Dark beaks and eyes concentrate interest on the heads and the posture of the birds themselves suggests devotion.

More about folding, cutting and composing

Many shapes are symmetrical and the simplest way of making them is often simply to fold then cut. The way to fold depends of course on the shape desired. Here, as a basis to work from, are three types of fold that often occur in this type of work particularly if the pattern is an individual one:

1. Simply fold the material or paper pattern in half (any thickness can be used for this), draw half the required shape and cut round both thicknesses of paper or material at once, leaving the centre fold intact (see top diagram). This method is suitable for flowers, grains, leaves, eggs, hearts and other such simple shapes. To get an idea of how the whole shape is going to look having drawn only half of it, hold the drawn half to a mirror at the centre line.

fold once

2. This involves folding the material twice or three times from the centre (see the two middle diagrams). Then draw a quarter or an eighth of the shape, depending on the number of times the material has been folded, and cut round this, again leaving the folded sides intact. This method is suitable for stars, squares, round flowers, hexagons, octagons etc. To get an impression of what the whole figure will look like use two mirrors and hold them at different angles from the drawing using the kaleidoscope principle. If the shape you are making requires several folds, make sure that all of them really do meet in the middle or the shape won't come out. Similarly, don't use too thick a fabric if you are going to fold it several times.

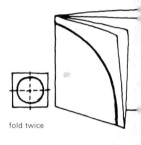
fold twice

3. The accordion fold (see diagrams below and bottom right). Simply fold the material accordion-fashion into as many layers as the thickness of the material (and the scissors) will allow. Draw half the figure and again cut round all thicknesses leaving the centre folds intact: the result will be a whole row of ships, dancing figures or whatever you have drawn, all joined together.

An inner and an outer shape can be made using any of the three methods of folding and cutting. If you do this the result, of course, will be a hole somewhere in the shape, under which a patch of a different colour or texture can be placed (see page 86).

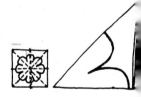
fold three times

Adding threads and beads

As you can see from the illustration above, a pattern may be embellished with threads or beads or, as in this case, both at the same time. Before adding anything of this nature it is wisest to have the finished work in front of you, preferably stretched over a frame or even hanging in its intended place.

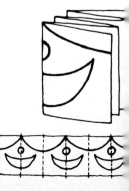

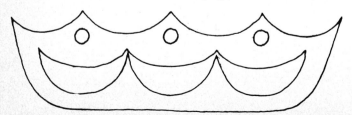

fold back and forth

Don't attempt to embellish your work in a half finished state, partly because you will not be able to judge the final effect, but also because adding adornments of this nature is very much a matter of experimenting to see what (if anything) sets off your work best, and you cannot experiment on a half-finished project.

Beads can either be strung on to a long thread which is then fixed to the work or fixed individually. Plastic ones will do, though again, it all depends very much on the project and colours involved: you may find buttons or sequins, for example, more suitable. Thread can either be used in conjunction with beads or alone, to delineate objects and achieve special effects. Again, the type of thread depends on the project: a gold or silver thread will show up well but may not be suitable for the pattern.

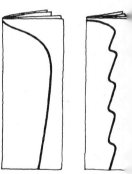

The diagrams above show how the patches are cut out, and the one below shows how the 'petals' are stitched to the base.

Putting petals in relief

A flower, for example, can be 'raised' from its background to achieve a more life-like three-dimensional effect by machine stitching layer upon layer of 'petal' patches, beginning at the outer edge (the outside petals), and machining only the inner edge of each petal. Cover the machining on the last circle of petals by sewing on a circular patch, as shown in the illustration. Leaves on the stalk of the flower can be fixed before the stalk

Above. Design with miners against a background of houses, mine and mountain showing good colour harmony in different parts of the design. The background is made up of rectangular patches, the figures are made of irregular patches; all are pasted on to a stiff material foundation.

Right. Wall hanging with rich, sparkling workmanship and colour. This is a fine example of how patches of different kinds can be arranged spontaneously in a unified pattern. The centre which is decorated with beads.

61

is sewn on so that the machining is subsequently hidden by the stalk. This technique can, of course, be adapted to other objects (see, for example, page 19). Details to be appliquéd in this way are best cut out double and the material stitched back to back from the inside and turned the right way out (so that the back of the petal is the same as the front) before being appliquéd.

Curtain in gay colours with flower cut-outs sewn with zigzag stitches on to broad-striped cotton.

Mounting and hanging wall decorations

As already demonstrated, different pieces of work are lined and mounted differently, depending on the project. Wall decorations, which frequently include irregular shapes as these allow the maximum scope for the imagination, are either glued or sewn on to a firm flat base and hung directly, or else mounted (either by glueing, sewing, or stretching and fixing over a firm backing)

*ght. Detail of the flower
own on page 60.*

and framed, either with or without glass, and then hung. You can either make the frame yourself (lengths of different varieties of beading can be bought at picture framing shops and glass can be bought cut to your own specifications from large ironmongers or glass merchants) or use an old frame housing an unwanted picture. If you do not intend to frame your decoration, it is often a good idea, depending on the materials used and the design, to insert wooden laths or metal poles into the hem at either end to keep the project flat.

Once mounted, the decoration can be hung by rings, cloth straps or hooks inserted in the top wooden lath. Similarly, curtains can also be hung by rings, cloth straps or one of the new devices continually appearing on the market.

Appliqué

This, one of the oldest forms of patchcraft, is the technique of sticking or stitching (literally 'applying') cut outs on to a background, as opposed to the more straightforward joining of one cut out to another which is, ordinary 'patchwork'. It can be used either in conjunction with ordinary patchwork (see the chapter 'Painting with Patches', in which the art of appliqué has already been touched on) or alone in a variety of methods offering much scope to the devotee of patchcraft. Appliqué has been used for centuries by many civilizations from the Incas, the so called 'Red' Indians to the people of the Far East. It was first introduced to Europe in medieval times, subsequently developed during the Renaissance and has proved popular ever since for all manner of projects from large decorative works of art to simple household objects. The method used depends largely on whether the project is to be purely decorative or also utilitarian.

Machine-sewn appliqué

Appliqué can be carried out either with the sewing machine or by hand. The former is obviously the quickest, and, now that the most expensive modern machines can manage practically all stitches previously carried out by hand, offers almost as wide a scope as hand sewing – providing the project is not too large for the machine. However, as few people own such a

Above. Detail of wall hanging on page 92. Patch with pointed corners are more easily appliquéd without turned-in edges, especially if the material is thick. Either machine or har stitch.

ake a cardboard pattern,
aw round its outline on to
ur material, then cut it out
owing for seams. Pin or
ck the material pattern on
its foundation or use a
itable tape. Using a zigzag
tch, sew the figure along
outline on to the
ckground and cut away
e seam allowance.
w a second time with a
der, close stitched seam.
more distinct outline is
us obtained by stitching
second seam over an
erted thread.

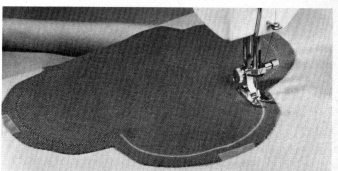

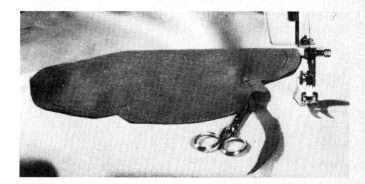

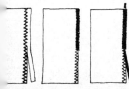

diagrams above illustrate
two machine seams.

signs for such a wall
nging as this can be taken
m drawings by children or
ılts, or from picture books.
e sketch above was made
erwards to show how a
ple drawing may become
appliqué design.

machine we shall deal in this section only with the stitches that can be carried out by an ordinary household sewing machine, that is, the normal machine stitch (backstitch) and a fine zig-zag stitch.

Use preferably a pliable material in a size which the machine can manage easily. Large projects are best made in sections by machine, doing the final sewing on by hand. 'Apply' the patches or cut outs either by turning in the edges and sewing a straight seam (the smaller the gauge used the less noticeable the seam will be though this will depend largely on the material used), or by sewing in 'zigzag' stitches over a clean cut un-turned edge, or by sewing in zigzag stitches over an outline drawn a little way inside the cut out, subsequently cutting away the superfluous material as close to the seam as possible. For a really neat finish this method demands a further stitching as shown in the bottom left hand diagram on page 65. As a rule the same colour of thread (an ordinary machine twist will do) is used throughout, though this, of course, depends on the design.

Wall hanging depicting a Scandinavian fairy-tale. The appliquéd pockets at the base of the wall hanging are edged with ribbon and have round holes, cords and tapes so that children can practise tying and knotting.

Raised appliqué.
The figures are sewn on to hessian using a zigzag stitch: small pleats give room for stuffing. Children appreciate prominent details such as the pinafore, the rings round the sun, the girl's streaming hair and her suspenders.

Designs using children's drawings

A good way to start on appliqué work is to use children's drawings, which often lend themselves beautifully to the craft and have a spontaneity and freshness not found in the work of older amateur draughtsmen. Try saving up several drawings and use each as a panel in a larger design — or, if you have a class of young children to teach, take one drawing from each child, cut out the patches and let the children do the appliqué work, using 'Cow gum' or some such adhesive.

Designs from children's books

Fairy tale characters make good subjects for appliqué. Either copy them freehand or use tracing paper, enlarging if necessary by the method described on page 52.

69

Designs using patterned materials

If you find the idea of drawing quite beyond your talents and if the idea of copying does not appeal (both, of course will take extra time) try the very old, widely used device of cutting out suitable patterns from pieces of material and appliquéing them — the textile equivalent of collage (see also page 64). The result can be most pleasing, as many fine well-preserved examples of quilts in museums will show. The effect is like embroidery, but of course the technique is much quicker and less skilful. Experiment with different textures and finishes as well as with colour and geometrical design. Silk, which was used as a background for the quilts referred to, makes a beautiful background for such cut outs with its softness and sheen, but as it is not the toughest of fabrics and can perish — not to mention its price — it is not always the best choice. The patterned patches themselves can be appliquéd either by machine (see page 64) or by hand (see page 74).

Designs for enlivening a child's bunk bed

Now for a particular project. As already demonstrated on page 33, children enjoy making miniature houses and playing in them, and a curtain draped round a bunk bed can keep a child amused for hours — particularly useful for rainy days, over-crowded homes or nursery schools. The most practical way of setting about making a bunk 'house' is to sew the curtain (any unused curtain or sheet will do) in sections, as shown in the diagram below. This makes for easier handling, fitting and washing. For a really firm 'wall' or whatever it is to be, add a lining to the outside material, sewing the two materials together with bias binding or ribbon — or simply machining them together. Once the 'base' has been made, sew on small patches to represent a post box, windows and so on, as shown in the illustration opposite.

How to make a puppet theatre and glove puppets

Page 33 demonstrates how a house made over a table can double up as a puppet theatre: a bunk bed 'house' is equally suitable for the job. Use the 'windows' as the stage and appliqué on a curtain which can rise and fall.

Now for the 'glove' or 'hand' puppets. These are simplicity itself to make. Use an old mitten or stocking as the base for both body and head or use the mitten or stocking for the body base and sew on a movable head made from parts of socks,

Diagrams showing how the 'bunk house' is made from five pieces. If the bed is in a corner (see illustration right) only four pieces are necessary. Measure the bed's width, length and from bunk to bunk for a complete 'house': the 'house' in the illustration is perhaps too short, but it is all a matter of individual preference.

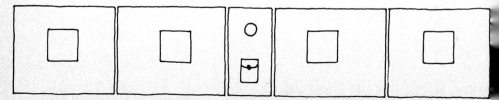

e sail cloth or some other
n cotton material if you
ven't an old curtain handy.
pliquéd figures and articles
p suggest an atmosphere.

gloves — anything pliable — making a hole for the middle fingers to push through and manipulate the puppet's 'head'. Appliqué on details such as ears, nose, eyes, again using any suitable material: felt is particularly good for the ears and nose or snout as it is stiff enough to stand out by itself; beads or buttons make splendid eyes. Appliqué on 'arms' made of fingers cut from old gloves, 'hands' of felt, again making holes so that the thumb and little finger can manipulate these. Clothes can be made and sewn on to the base to disguise it and, if desired, identify the puppet. Machining is the quickest and easiest way of appliquéing on the details: let the children themselves help by choosing the materials, hunting out odds and ends, glueing and, if old enough, sewing as well.

Left. A surface covered with daisies. Cut out the right number of flowers and leaves and arrange them so that they just overlap, then machine them on to the background material using a zigzag stitch. The actual surface is large so the rather frayed edges are not noticeable.

Right, and left in detail. A rich and subtly varied pattern of leaves and flowers using fabrics with and without a pattern, some thin, others closely woven. The outlines have been oversewn by hand because it is easy to stitch round the leaves in a variety of colours.

Hand sewn appliqué

Hand sewing offers a greater variation of stitches than the ordinary household sewing machine; it is essential for large or complicated projects; it is also more restful. Work with a frame for ease and best results.

Sewing small patches on to a large one

The tree-top in the illustration above stands out as a whole rather than a mass of small patches owing not only to the use of light patches at the top graduating to darker ones at the bottom, but also to the single large patch of tulle on to which the 'leaves' have been overcast by hand to blend them with the foundation material while keeping their individual shapes. This use of a large 'under patch' is worth remembering for such designs.

Embroidery for edging patches

By the use of embroidery stitches you can avoid the tedious task of turning in and hemming individual patches for appliqué. This *can* be done by machine (see page 64), but is usually done by hand, sewing the patch directly on to the background. First fix the patch to be appliquéd with tape, pins or tacking, then embroider it on, choosing one of the commonly used stitches demonstrated in the diagrams on the right. There are both wide and narrow stitches to choose from, depending partly on the effect you wish to achieve and how strongly the outline is to be depicted, and partly on how easily the fabric frays. Each stitch varies in the time taken to sew and amount of thread used: quickest is the most commonly used overcasting, which is usually carried out over a turned edge or machine seam.

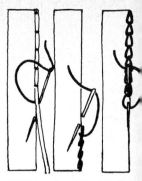

oversewing, stem stitch, chain stitch

herringbone, feather stitch, buttonhole stitch

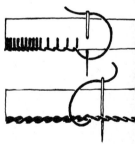

close and open buttonholing, braid stitch

Left. Coarse fabric makes a good background for cotton appliqué work. For this wall hanging two different bird patterns were used; most of them were sewn on with chain stitch, some with stem stitch and some were pasted on. Right above. Detail.

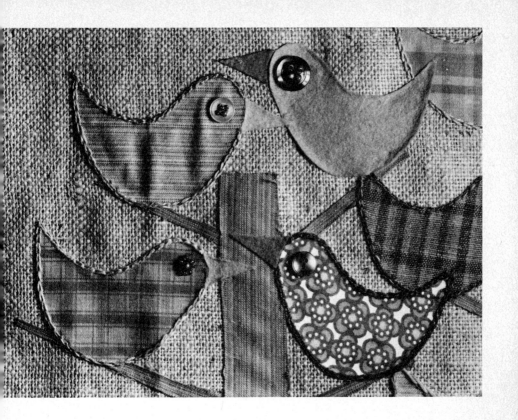

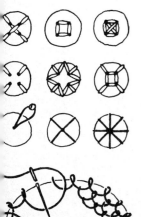

Buttons, beads, spangles, glass

In appliqué designs beads and spangles of all sorts are often used to make raised and sparkling details. They can mark out flower centres, form fruits on a tree or be sewn on as eyes. Buttons can be used in the same way. Bits of glass, wood, mirrors or thin stones can also be used in appliqué: fix them first with tape or a little paste, then sew them over and over in layers to make a network to hold them firm. Other thin objects can be held firm in roughly the same way.

The diagrams, left, demonstrate how buttons and spangles can be sewn on. Either sew them with as thin a thread as possible in the same colour as the button or spangle, or else make a bold contrast to show off the stitches to effect. Small details such as these may even serve a practical purpose; they, could, for example, hold several layers of material together, possibly with padding in between.

Another way of sewing on spangles, buttons and large beads is demonstrated in the top two birds' eyes illustrated above; the thread has been sewn up and down to fill out the button's 'eye' and a bead has been sewn on to the top to take the place of a knot.

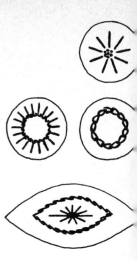

stitches which both fasten and decora[te]

*Left. An attractive wall
hanging with a disciplined
use of colour: greyish-white
base with brown, green, pin[k]
and a little blue. The materia[l]
on the other hand are of
various types, some with
woven patterns. Little by litt[le]
details are discovered such [as]
the vehicle in the distance b[y]
the wood and the flower on
the bench. Opposite. Details*

Using patches as a base for embroidery

This is a speedier way of obtaining a richly embroidered effect
than using embroidery alone. The patch gives an impression of
distance and the embroidery consequently stands out, almost
covering the patches. Choose smooth, unpatterned materials
and a suitably neutral tone of colour. If you intend to make
your work washable, do not forget to test the patches for
colour fastness by dipping them in a warm soapy water solution

suitable for washing and then rubbing them on white material. Remember also to preshrink all the patches used (*before* cutting them out) as well as the foundation material. Pressing must also be given careful attention. Most types of embroidery will only bear careful pressing on the wrong side and against a soft underlay. They should be damped before being stretched flat. Only when they have been pressed should the patches be tacked in place. If you have not been using a frame, begin in the middle and work towards the edges to avoid wrinkling and unnecessary fraying. Embroidery should also be done in that order to keep it in shape.

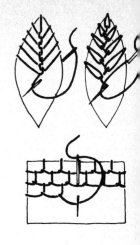

How to transfer appliqué shapes on to background material

It is sometimes necessary, particularly in complex designs, to draw the shape to be appliquéd, even the embroidery as well, on to both the foundation material and the material to be used for the patch itself. If you are using thin, light materials, or any material with a degree of transparency, simply trace straight on to the material from a pattern placed underneath. On closely woven, smooth materials try depicting the pattern by sticking pins through the outline on to the material. The small holes left will often be a sufficient guide and this method is infinitely quicker than resorting to copying paper. If, however, you have to use copying paper, place it between the pattern paper and material, using a dark paper for transfer to light material and light to transfer to dark. Be careful that the copying paper does not make unwanted marks on the material. If you have no copying paper handy, colour the reverse of the pattern paper with a medium-soft pencil and then draw in the lines with a hard pencil as if you were using ordinary copying paper. An alternative to simply sticking pins through the outline on to the material is to produce holes along the lines of the pattern, then place the pattern on the material and press a mixture of dye-powder and talc through the holes with the aid of a cotton-wool pellet, or something similar. Another fairly simple method which can sometimes be applied is to cut out paper models in thin cardboard, place them on the material and draw round the outline with a fine-pointed pencil. If the shape had to be placed on the appliquéing material in a particular way, for example if the material is patterned and a particular part of the pattern (a flower, for example, or a leaf) must come in the centre of the shape, then use a stiff transparent paper for cutting out the models.

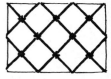

Colour surfaces can be decorated with embroidery thin thread or thin wool as shown above. The result is rather like a small-patterned material.

Top right. 'Painted' scene of a patch surface. For this, a colour slide or picture postcard could be copied. The printed woven patterns add to the liveliness of the gaily coloured picture, with its small cottages down by the lake and tall houses in the distance.

Bottom right. Nursery wall depicting a railway through summer landscape. The rail are made of striped materia. The hanging has many pockets to put things into and one tree has hooks und the foliage. Make the hang by preshrinking each patch and testing it for colour-fastness before machine-stitching it with double he

Hemming appliqué patches

If you wish to make a particularly neat finish by turning in or hemming a patch then it must be cut out with a hem allowance. You can make this very narrow if the material is thin and does not fray easily, but if in doubt, allow for a wider edge at first

The design above uses
patches as a coloured surface
on which to embroider. The
delicate embroidery makes
the patches show up well on
a thin fabric. Threaded,
crocheted or quilted details
can sometimes be used as
decoration.

Right. A wall hanging.
A colourful appliqué design
with flowers and leaves
framed in material with
interwoven metallic threads.

details from the colour
tration opposite: a white
h in a closely woven
c on a white, open-weave
ground is depicted by
well-stitched embroidery
h also serves to form a
sition between the two
rials.

and cut away the superfluous, if any, later. If you are using a thin and easily frayed material, mount it on an adhesive 'stick-on' material before cutting out.

There are various ways of turning in the edges. If you are using a firm cotton material, press the edge down with an iron round a cardboard model as for ordinary patchwork (see page 13). Be careful with models made from transparent material, as they will not stand much heat. Then, if necessary, pin or tack the seam allowance on to the patch without the model. It is often advisable, however, to place the patches on to the background material *before* the hem allowance is turned in. If you do this, first pin or tack the patch a good way inside its outline, before moving the pins or tacks carefully into the right position, at the same time checking size and fit. If a patch is to cover another partially, do not turn in the edge on the hidden portion, as this would make for extra bulk. Leave in any necessary tacking stitches until the design is finally sewn, removing them before pressing or damp stretching. Whether the hem allowance is turned in before or after the placing on the material, trim away any superfluous material with scissors, especially in the pointed outside corners. Cut away small triangles where the turned-in seam makes lumps, for example round convex curves. Make small notches to prevent straining at the edge of the material where the pattern has concave curves and corners. Once the edge in question has been turned in and trimmed, either invisibly stitch it on to background material or use some sort of decorative edge (see page 74). In some cases you will need to use two or more different methods in conjunction. For instance an overcasting does not fasten the patch very well, but does form an attractive outline. The best method of 'invisible stitching' is to make small backstitches close to the edge in the same colour as the material.

Quilts, pillows, pot-holders and so on may be decorated with appliqué work then quilted according to the directions on pages 42 and 43. In view of washing and wear and tear the edges of the patches should be turned in properly on such items. The stitches fastening the patches can function as quilting and keep various layers of stuff and padding in place at one and the same time.

On pages 55 and 56 an account is given of how large-size objects can be built up from patches laid one after another like petals, feathers or scales, then sewn on one after another all with a turned-in edge. For such projects it is best to finish sewing the whole large appliquéd shape first, then turn in the outer edges of the large shape and appliqué it on to the background material.

As very small patches are difficult to turn in, always sew them on instead with a suitable edging stitch, for example, bottonhole stitch or satin stitch. An attractive alternative is to replace the whole patch with a piece of embroidery. Such details draw attention to themselves, and can thus be used to accentuate certain parts of a design.

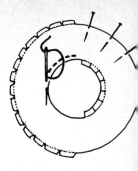

Cut out notches or triangles according to the shape

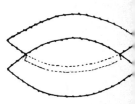

If one patch overlaps another the he of the covered part is not turned in

Invisible oversewing and back stitch

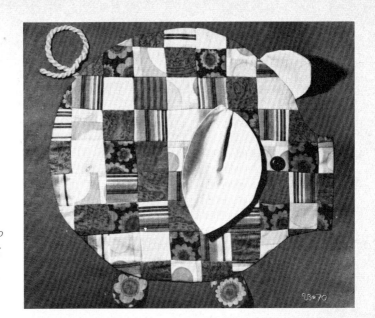

Patchwork pig converted into appliqué design. On large, round shapes a hem is easily turned in. Details such as ears and feet can be turned twice to make them stand out from the background.

Cockerel made of patches of highly-coloured silk appliquéd on to a dark background.

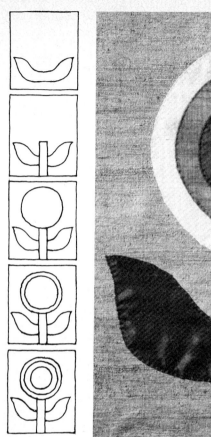

ove right. Flower made of
mmed silk patches sewn
to the background with
all backstitches and
rsewing. The diagrams
ve show how patch is
on patch.

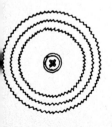

old-fashioned pen-wiper
inspire ideas for
hions.

Sewing patch on patch

In the past, penwipers were made from small variegated patches in cloth, felt or some similar material. They were often cut with a zigzag edge into circles, hearts or flowers. As a rule they were composed of patches decreasing in size, so that the various colours showed up, and finished with a button in the centre. Appliqué can be carried out in the same way. Begin with a large patch and gradually build on smaller and smaller patches, either in the same or a different shape. Place each patch centrally over the next or over its edge. A circular design such as the flower above will make a cushion decoration if you discard the leaves and stalk. The largest circle has been drawn round a fruit dish, the others round a plate, a saucer and a pot-lid. Exchange circles for hearts, squares or other simple shapes. Practically any material may be used — the most important consideration is colour. For such practical projects always hem the edges to avoid fraying.

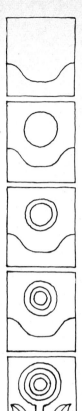

stitch the low
patch on to t
upper one

cut a hole.
put a patch
underneath i
and sew firm

cut a smaller
hole, put and
patch under
sew firm

cut a still
smaller hole,
put another
patch under
it

cut out the v
design in a p
large enough
be placed ov
the other,
built-up patc

Putting a patch under a hole

The technique used for patching the knees of trousers, putting a patch under the hole and sewing it on, can be adapted for use in appliqué work. The patch may be made from one piece of material or from several pieces in different colours sewn together. A leaf, for example, could be given a seam down the centre. For this, stitch together two sufficiently large patches, press the seam flat and place the patch under a leaf-shaped hole. Invisible stitches are best for keeping the notched and turned-in edges firm. Patch and cut out material must be placed so that both weaves run the same way. If the first patch is a large one, you could cut out holes in decreasing sizes and put patches underneath each hole, rather than cut out one large hole and fill it with one large patch. For this technique do buttonhole stitching over the edge of the thread or use a material that does not fray. The technique is a particularly good one for making cushions with large simple designs.

Above left. Silk appliqué hemmed in invisible oversewing. The diagrams above show the order in which the work is carried o (see colour illustration on back cover).

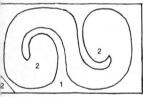
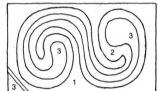

e diagrams above
monstrate how to cut
terns in three layers of
terial, leaving a fourth
er intact. For this design
backs of worn-out shirts
d blouses were used; the
ge was turned in and
nmed with invisible back
ching.

Cutting holes in holes

For the flower illustrated opposite, material was gradually cut
away and patches placed underneath. The 'cutting-through' or
'mola' technique as it is also called (the word comes from the
Indian women in the San Blas Islands who use it for their
blouses, 'molas') uses more or less the same method. These
'molas' are made of thin cotton material in several differently
coloured layers. Tack all the different coloured pieces of
material together, having first cut them all to the same size.
Cut large patterns out of the top piece and hem the edges, then
cut new, smaller holes through the next layer of material and
so on until only one layer remains. Three to four layers give a
very rich pattern effect if the possibilities of the technique are
well exploited. If you intend to hem the edges, use a closely
woven, not too thick material. For a really firm finish make the
stitches which fasten down the edges also act as quilting, that
is, make them penetrate all the layers of material.

Ribbons and patches

Ribbons and decorative edgings can be used together with patches in several ways and sewn on in larger or smaller lengths instead of pieces of material. As they only need to be turned-in at the ends, are easy to sew, and strong, ribbons are quick and easy to work with. Either place them straight on a background or if both sides of the ribbon are alike they can be turned at the corners, otherwise turn them in one or other of the ways shown in the diagrams. Sew them on either by machine or by hand, with seams along the edges or in the centre. using small 'invisible' or decorative stitching.

Ribbon can also be used at the edge of patches to mark the transition between two colours or textures, but its most practical use is for binding raw edges. Let them cover the join between two patches or place them over the edge of an un-hemmed appliqué patch. Ribbon is particularly suitable for use on machine-washed articles such as quilted covers, cushions, pot-holders, curtains and clothes, but the ribbons *must* be shrunk first and checked for colour fastness (see page 8).

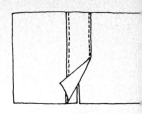

place a ribbon over the join

sew along edge of ribbon

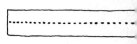

sew along centre of ribbon

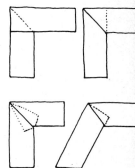

make accurate corners

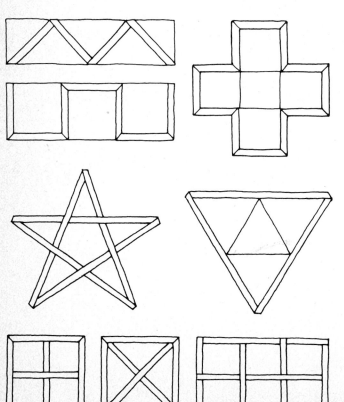

The diagrams left show how patches may be bound in various ways with ribbon. This applies to both hemmed and unhemmed material patches forming whole surfaces, borders or individual designs. Some of the diagrams may give ideas for window stars or mobile hanging decorations, pot-holders and small tablecloth

ll hanging in a mixture of
hniques. Longer and
rter pieces of ribbon and
id against a background
patches contribute greatly
he lively effect of the
ole.

Patterned ribbon. Small pieces of embroidered ribbon are very useful for details in many designs. On houses they can be windows, doors, railings. Scraps of lace and embroidery can also be used. It's quicker to sew on such details than to embroider them, and the result can be much the same.

Left. Detail showing how patches with edges (hems) turned in were oversewn on to a background using a light-coloured thread. Pieces of all kinds of ribbon can be used to advantage for small and rectangular details.

Tie- and batik-dyed patchwork

...autifully designed and ...vn appliqué depicting ...ses at the water's edge. ...tice the alteration between ...t and dark houses and the ...iation in details. It is easy ...imagine the design in ...ours.

If you practice tie-dyeing or batik work, take advantage of your dye bath to push in a few patches or piece of material for patchwork at the same time: they will always come in handy even if you haven't a particular project in mind. If you don't practise one of these crafts but would like to obtain the beautiful nuances of colour obtainable by home dyeing, simply buy one of the home dyeing kits on the market (a cold water dye is particularly good as it is both colour- and light-fast) and follow the instructions carefully for making the dye. Then tie your piece of material into knots, fold it into triangles and put a rubber band over the end of each angle, tie thread or string round it at intervals (don't be afraid to experiment with a combination of these tie-dye ideas or with ideas of your own) or alternatively wax a pattern on to it (for this you will need wax,

a dropper and preferably a handbook on batik as the technique is more complicated than that of tie-dye), then dip it once for the time stated in the dye or dip it several times either in the same dye or in one of a different colour, drying and rinsing the material (removing any wax) and re-knotting, re-tying or re-waxing it differently between each dye.

Mixing techniques

Don't be afraid of experimenting with various combinations of techniques and materials, working out practical easy ways of treating details. Try, for example, working on a foundation of dark and light patches sewn together and appliquéing patches, ribbons, cords and embroidery on to it. Attractive three-dimensional effects can be obtained, especially if the appliquéd details are placed partly over one another, so that they appear

This composition may inspi both children and adults to start sewing, either in a group or separately.
If working in a group you will often find that one person finds it easiest to cu out figures while another finds it easiest to embroider and so on.

in relief. Don't forget the part that dark and light colours and wide and narrow strips play in creating an impression of perspective. In stylistically decorative compositions which allow the individual a free interpretation of the work, such details are particularly important. The illustration on page 89, for example, can be interpreted as either an interior or an exterior — a street or factory, perhaps, with its associations of light and sound.

Make full use of buttons, buckles and other such devices mentioned throughout the book: the appliqué illustration opposite, for example, has doors and windows to open and shut, showing activities in and around the house. Many details of this illustration could, with simple changes, form a whole design (see above).

Left and below. Details of composition on page 92. The doors and windows are cut double and sewn up preferably with stiffening between inner and outer material.

Right. A detail which shows many different ways of self-expression using pieces of material, leather, embroidery and yarn.

A final word of advice . . .

Above all, have fun with the patches you cut out and use to create designs. If you don't the result is bound to be boring, whereas plenty of enthusiasm usually works wonders with even the most limited amount of knowledge and craftsmanship. If working alone bores you, invite a friend or friends to join in the work (or, if you're a teacher, let the whole class join in) and make a communal effort: the result is often highly imaginative, exciting and unexpected — it's also much quicker! Don't be put off by the amount of time your first efforts may take: remember that with a little practice you will get along much faster, and as your skill increases, so too will your interest in the craft. Finally, don't forget that this is meant to be a guide for the beginner and a guide and inspiration to the more advanced, so treat it as such: make it a jumping off point rather than a textbook which must be followed at all times, for the craft itself is only limited by the bounds of the craftsman's imagination.

Index